Books by Ray Hollenbach

The Impossible Mentor: Finding Courage to Follow Jesus

25 Days of Christmas

One Month of Thanksgiving

50 Forgotten Days

The Man With All The Answers

Deeper
GRACE

Published by Lone Valley Publishing,
Campbellsville, KY 42718

Cover photo by Darren Moore
http://www.darrenmoorephotography.com/
Used by his kind permission.

For
Joe & Laura,
Evangeline,
and Kate-Lin.

Each one a grace gift.

Table of Contents

Breathe Deep

Too often we have shortened grace into a simple retelling of forgiveness, but it's so much more. Like the atmosphere, it surrounds all creation. Grace is the atmosphere of our life with God. Each moment we breathe, we breathe deep of grace. And just as we are unaware of our breathing, a vast amount of God's grace goes unnoticed. We would cease to exist without grace.

This small book will help you breathe.

You're already breathing. You're going to breathe whether you choose to or not. But sometimes we need to simply stop and take a deep breath. Or two. Or three. Each entry in this book is a breath.

Have you ever thought about breathing? We inhale fresh air; we fill our lungs with our most vital need. This clean air carries life-giving oxygen. Our lungs take the oxygen and—somehow, miraculously—give the oxygen to each red blood cell. The life-giving air has now become mixed into our bloodstream. Arteries carry the oxygen—the air we breathed just moments ago—to every corner of our body. Every cell receives oxygen. Our cells could not function without its steady stream.

And something more happens. Deep inside us each cell gives away whatever is old and dirty. Arteries become veins, and those same cells carry away the waste, back to the lungs. We exhale, and rid ourselves of what we no longer need.

Physicians call this respiration, but it's really grace, God's grace, played out 20,000 times a day. That's how often (and how deeply) we need that grace.

Why Grace Means Something More Than Forgiveness

Once upon a time there was an abusive husband. He was a rage-aholic, given to fits of anger and, horribly, those moments sometimes overflowed into violence. Like the time he slammed his wife up against the kitchen cabinets. Or the time he slapped her across the face and then, in horror and shame, he ran off to find a quiet place to tremble and cry.

The wife—a Christian—forgave her husband each time he came home. He said (quite accurately), "I don't know what comes over me." The wife loved her husband deeply and saw the many good sides of this flawed man, but she lived in fear that the next rage-riot might bring a harm that would not heal. She stayed with her husband because each time he sincerely begged for forgiveness. She knew her duty as Christian was to extend grace.

The only thing she knew of God's grace was forgiveness. She had been told all her life that she herself was powerless over sin, and God's grace came to forgive and restore her relationship with God. She was enough of a Christian to understand that if God had forgiven her, she should extend the same grace to others, especially her husband.

She knew a small piece of God's grace, but only enough to put her in danger.

It's God's grace that forgives and restores. Sweet forgiveness. Sweet—and filled with torment unless there is something more. If we look at the wife in this story we want to scream, "Get out! It's not safe!" Any sane Christian understands the woman has no duty to remain at home and risk injury or death because of some notion of grace, expressed as constant forgiveness.

If we look at the husband in this story we see a man trapped in thoughts, emotions, and behaviors that will harm everyone he loves and ruin his own life as well. A sympathetic view of the husband understands he, too, is a tormented soul in desperate need of help—help beyond merely wiping clean his sinful slate. The most gracious thing his wife could do would be to move out and demand that he get the help he needs to overcome his deep anger and pain.

And what of Jesus, the third member of the marriage? We could no more imagine Jesus leaving this husband in his condition than we could imagine Jesus telling a homeless man, "Go your way, be warm and filled" without giving him food and clothing.

Beyond the characters in this simple story lies a larger question: what about us? Would a grace-filled God leave us in the condition he finds us? Would he spend his days reminding us of our shortcomings, demanding again and again prayers of repentance and sorrow? Would the loving Creator wave his hand and say, "you are forgiven, now—go and sin no more" without lifting even one finger to empower us over our sin?

Sometimes an extreme example is necessary to grab our hearts and free our minds. Does God's grace mean only forgiveness, or is there something more to his antidote for sin? Would God leave us alone in our rage, our addictions, or our isolation? A cold and comfortless God he would be if it were so.

The problem is not with the Father, nor his grace: it is *our understanding* of grace—of God's on-going work in our lives. Jesus will not leave us to ourselves any more than he would leave a beggar in the street. Anyone who suggests so misrepresents the true grace of God.

Set aside the question of Heaven or Hell after we die: what about Heaven or Hell while we live? The fabric of everyday life is alive with the grace of God. Grace forgives, but it also guides. If we wait until we've sinned to call upon the grace of God, we've squandered the greater part of grace. Grace restores, but it also guards. It also instructs us to deny ungodly ways and teaches us the *how-to* of life: how to life sensible, upright, and godly lives in this present age.

The scripture teaches we are saved by grace. The good news is we can experience salvation here-and-now as well as there-and-then. The Kingdom of Heaven glides on wings of grace. The Kingdom brings righteousness, peace, and joy—and best of all the gracious Holy Spirit leads us to these three in everyday life. The Kingdom is never attained; it is received. How will we receive the grace of the Kingdom today?

A Stingy Granny is an Oxymoron

Let us sing today in praise of grandmothers. Those loving, accepting, wiser-than-they-let-on souls who never stop welcoming you no matter what your age. They feed you at the drop of a napkin and pile your plate high with food prepared by ethereal love. Grandma would never think of holding back the mashed potatoes. She'll give you a portion obscenely large, carbohydrates mountain-high, flowing with gravy rivers.

A stingy granny is an oxymoron, a sad misfit of nature. Honestly, who thinks their grandmother wouldn't give all she had? And yet, beloved as she might be, your grandmother doesn't set a table like Jesus.

Consider these few words from Ephesians: *"But to each one of us grace has been given as Christ apportioned it."* (4:7) Now stop and ask: what kind of portion would Jesus give? No one has trouble imagining the goodness of grandma. Why then is it so hard to imagine the grace of God flowing out in portions high and deep, prepared in a kitchen where the supply never ends and the Master Chef knows our every need?

Read it again: *"But to each one of us grace has been given as Christ apportioned it."* So many of us stumble on the word "*apportion.*" We let our fears tell us that Jesus will somehow hold something back because of our boneheaded behavior or headstrong ways. We are tempted to think he will only feed us when we've been good.

"Ahem, ahem," says the short theologian with a flower in her hat. "Paul is talking about gifts like apostle, prophet, evangelist, pastor or teacher. Always read the context," she says. "Paul is talking about how Jesus provides for the church. It's a specific kind of grace. We should not expect he gives everyone the same portion." This is how the confining logic of loveless interpretation begins to close us in.

Perhaps, I say. Perhaps that's true. Except I've supped at his table, I've feasted with him in the here-and-now before his great marriage feast has gotten underway. I can tell you he piles the grace high and deep. Not just forgiving grace: he ladles out grace for hope, grace for starting again, grace for growth, the grace of leadership, community, love, and vision. He makes new wine for those who have already had too much. He feeds multitudes and leaves baskets more behind.

If the theologian in the flowered hat needs a greater context for the verse in Ephesians, I choose these reminders:

> *"He who did not spare his own Son, but gave him up for us all—how will he not also, along with him, graciously give us all things?"* (Romans 8:32)

—or—

> *"Out of his fullness we have all received grace in place of grace already given."* (John 1:16)

If you have trouble with the idea that Christ apportions grace, perhaps it's because those who taught you have lost sight of what size portions Jesus gives. Here's a joyful mediation: imagine the Lord of glory ringing the dinner bell on the front porch, calling out across the ranch:

> *Ho! Everyone who's thirsty, come to the waters; and you who have no money, come, buy and eat! Come, buy wine and milk without money and without cost.* (Isaiah 55:1)

Jesus might even ask your grandma to help serve up the feast.

EXERCISE: GREATER GRACE

TAKE TEN MINUTES:

Be still. Invite the Holy Spirit to come near. Breathe.

(Don't hurry. Wait until you're confident the Spirit is poised to help you in this exercise.)

Pray: "Spirit of God, please open my eyes and heart to recognize your grace-works in my life."

Listen: As you pray, you may think your mind is wandering, but take note of the memories and thoughts that come to mind.

Ask Yourself: Has God prompted me toward a larger understanding of grace?

Write: Make a few notes of what came to your mind. What did you discover about God in these ten minutes? What did you discover about yourself?

TAKE TEN WEEKS:

What might happen if you tried this exercise once a week, for ten weeks? This exercise (like the others in this small book) is not about getting the right answer. It's about opening our eyes, ears, and lives to the deeper grace God has in store.

The Small-Minded Judge

Here's my story: I grew up in a Roman Catholic home, but became an Evangelical during my teenage years. I used to think this was so clever: later, when I became a Protestant pastor I would refer to Roman Catholics as our "cousins." I thought this cute phrase highlighted our close association with Catholics while subtly reminding the listener of the differences between the great Reformation divide. Those Catholics are family, but only cousins. Pretty witty, eh? Not really. I'm ashamed to say that I did this for years.

Eventually the still small voice of the Spirit began to get through. *"Really, Ray? Do you really mean to say these people do not have the same Father?"* I tried to argue with the voice for a while. "These people have such different practices." I answered. "Their church is full of cultural influences that have nothing to do with the Scripture." Case made, right?

The Spirit's voice is gentle, but strong: it's a velvet granite breath. *"And your church? Don't your practices seem strange to Baptists or Presbyterians? And what about the cultural influences in your church? Perhaps the Apostle Paul would have a thing or two to say about them?"* Eventually I acknowledged that the billion-plus people who are Catholics are part of God's family. They are brothers and sisters, who call Jesus Lord and King. My opinions of their practices did not matter. God's opinion does.

Then a marvelous thing happened. I discovered the divine banqueting table was longer than I had imagined. It stretched beyond my fleshly vision. I discovered I had been invited to come and feast, not criticize. I beheld sisters and brothers I had never known before. If I revered the Father why not revere the family?

And one more thing happened. A spirit of criticism began to lift from my mind. The real issue had never been about Protestants and Catholics. The issue was my critical, demanding heart. The issue was my self-appointed position as the judge over all God's kingdom—such a big kingdom, and such a small-minded judge! I no longer felt the need to walk the police beat of orthodoxy. If a few impostors came to the feast, I knew the Father could choose who should eat and who would be shown the door. I was free to find the best in people and ignore their flaws. The same Spirit who corrected me could correct them.

Grace asks: is it possible we criticize other Christians publicly because inwardly we don't see them as family?

Grace Confronts

What is the distance between you and God? The answer is always "not far." When the Apostle Paul spoke to a group of people in Athens (pagans who were completely alienated for God) he told them "*He is not far from any one of us.*" Where did he get such an idea? Of course, he got it from God. Consider his personal story.

If there was ever a candidate for the wrath of God, Paul's your man: a Jew who had rejected the Messiah; a religious cop bent on dragging apostate Hebrews back to Jerusalem to face the music. The Lord Jesus took Paul's persecution of the people of the church personally, asking, "Why have you persecuted *me?*" When Jesus met Paul on the road to Damascus it was a confrontation of grace, not judgment. By confronting Paul, Jesus lived out his own parable: the good shepherd left the ninety-nine and went after the one who had wandered away.

Imagine Paul, struck blind, sitting alone in a strange city, forced to re-think his religious convictions. He had given his life to the study of the Hebrew Scriptures. He was considered a rising star in Judaism. He had been taught by the best rabbis and put his faith into action as an orthodox bounty hunter. Then, after encountering Jesus personally, he sat in darkness and wrestled with one thought: *everything I know is wrong.* Then came divine healing, divine instruction, and divine appointments. Years later, as Paul stood at the marketplace of ideas in Athens, he suggested his story is everyone's story: the sensual, the cerebral, the religious, the skeptic, the clueless and the pagan. Paul could say so because he had experienced the reality. All it takes is one real encounter with Jesus to make us re-think our ideas about God. Not religious argument or philosophical persuasion, but encounter.

Years ago I experienced an encounter with God. It was quite nearly a Damascus road experience: as I drove cross-country on an Interstate highway, he spoke to me so clearly I thought there was someone else in the car: "Ray, I want you to reconsider everything in your life except being born again, and being married." The idea was startling, but it lead me in new directions of church planting, pastoring, and writing this very book.

The grace of God confronts each of us personally. The Bible has recorded such grace-confrontations since the book of Genesis:

§ After Adam and Eve choose to eat from the tree of knowledge of good and evil they discovered their nakedness and tried to hide from God. Far from rejecting them, God himself went searching for them. "Adam!" he cried, "Where are you?"

§ When Cain was angry with his brother it was Yahweh who tried to talk him down from the ledge. Even after the murder of Abel, God not only heard the voice of the victim, he placed a mark of protection on the oppressor.

§ When Jacob cheated his brother and lied to his father, God did not reject him (though it would have been understandable). Instead,

25

God revealed Himself at Bethel and said, *"I am with you and will watch over you wherever you go . . . I will not leave you until I have done what I have promised you." (Genesis 28:15)*

The story of Israel goes on and on: each chapter reveals that God himself is the seeker: his people are the sought.

By the time Paul had re-calibrated his understanding of God, he was able to celebrate God's goodness and affections: *"For I am convinced that neither death nor life, neither angels nor demons, neither the present nor the future, nor any powers, neither height nor depth, nor anything else in all creation, will be able to separate us from the love of God that is in Christ Jesus our Lord."* (Romans 8:38-39) Paul, the legalist, had become an apostle—not only of God's grace—but of his presence and goodness as well.

Paul understood that the Father always wants to be among us, and he will not allow anything to get in the way. If sin separates us from the Father, then the Father provides a remedy. It's more than a legal transaction: the record shows that God will go to any length to be with us. If, as Isaiah says, *"your iniquities have separated you from your God; your sins have hidden his face from you,"* (Isaiah 59: 2) it is because we are the ones in hiding. He has not gone anywhere. He is still *"not far from any one of us."*

I wonder now how many of us need time and space to re-calibrate our view of the Father. How many of the

26

events in our personal history point to God's desire to be with us (if only the scales would fall from our eyes)?

The Divine Scandal

Is there anything more irresponsible than grace? It's the refuge of losers, the hiding place of the harebrained, the only hope at end of the line. How do we learn anything from grace if we are shielded from the fruit of our ways? How can we grow into responsible adults if we are allowed to avoid the shipwreck of our poor choices?

Better to live well grounded in the predictable world of choice and consequence. Consequence is the lever of choice, tilting upon the worldly fulcrum of cause and effect; sowing and reaping are the dependable laws of nature. Karma chants responsibility: "Choose, and eat the fruit of your choice." How can we mature apart from learning the mathematics of choice and consequence?

To look at grace from the outside is to see how rogues get off scot-free. The work of grace is the spoiling of an only child. Grace runs counter to good stewardship. Grace is the foolishness of giving a field hand a full day's pay for but a few hours work.

Oh, but from the inside—to taste of grace is to drink the water of life. It's the meal without the tab. The drinks are on the house. Grace is more and better wine even though the guests are tipsy. Grace is calories that somehow don't count. Karma is the voice of reason; grace is the voice of love. And here is our dilemma: we want grace for ourselves, but choose Karma for others. The trick is to see grace from the inside—on behalf of others.

Simone Weil said there are but two forces capable of moving the human heart: gravity and grace. Gravity, the great force of nature, exerts its unstoppable influence from the outside; grace, the beautiful power of super nature, lifts our hearts until we float on air. Reason cautions us that grace is dangerous: the unscrupulous can figure the con quickly. Grace can be abused, grace can be played the fool, grace can be wasted.

But grace doesn't care. Grace is the divine scandal. Grace is the way of Heaven, where mercy triumphs over judgment: not that judgment is unknown, but that judgment itself has been tried and found wanting.

Grace is more than a gift; it is the example of Heaven. Grace is the way, the truth, and the life. Grace calls us not only to taste and see, but also to come and follow. The grand goal of grace is that we would not be mere partakers, but that we would become the servants in its grand banquet. Grace calls us to fill the glass of every thirsty soul.

Unlimited Grace, Limited Me

How big is grace? Grace is scattered like stars on a cloudless night. Grace is fathomless as the ocean depths. Grace inexhaustible, grace forever fresh, grace boundless and free. And yet hidden in the abundance of grace lays a danger to my soul.

The problem is not God's supply of grace. Infinite God, infinite grace. The problem is me: tiny, finite, limited, breakable me. Here's the contrast, and also the danger: God is infinite but the human psyche is not.

Two examples: author Philip Yancey tells a first-hand story of his friend who was thinking about an extra-marital affair. "What I want to know," asked the friend "is if I go ahead and do this: will God forgive me?" Yancey, stunned, finally hears the Spirit whisper, and he answers: "The question is not whether God will forgive, but whether you will want his forgiveness." The dreadful results played out. The man had the affair; his marriage dissolved; and he walked away from his identity as a follower of Jesus. Dallas Willard teaches the same lesson when he reminds us that although God's love, grace, and mercy are without limit the human heart will only bend so far before it breaks.

Like a man I knew who inherited a million dollars and wasted it all in carelessness and foolish desires, the wealth of grace reveals the hidden desires of our hearts. What if we love sin more than grace? Martin Luther famously challenged us, *"Be a sinner and sin boldly, but believe and rejoice in Christ even more boldly"* but he presumed the sinner's heart was still turned toward

God. What if we sin not in boldness, but in complete disregard for the love of God and his work of restoration? What if sin is the true desire of our soul?

John's gospel opens with words of grace: "From the fullness of his grace we have all received one blessing after another." (John 1:16) Apparently the good folks who translated the New International Version were challenged by the more literal rendering of this verse, "From his fullness we have all received, grace upon grace." (New Revised Standard Version). The NIV substitutes "one blessing after another" for "grace upon grace." But why argue over translation? I believe John was searching for a way to communicate that God's grace is multi-layered. If we walk with him 50 years we will discover again and again the God who beckons us (in C.S. Lewis' happy phrase) to come "farther up and farther in." But take note: if we are determined to think of grace as merely a ticket to heaven there is no farther up and farther in—either in this life or the next. Why come to the shores of God's grace only to dip our toes in the ocean?

The Dance of Grace

Last year I saw a professional dancer dance. I sat just ten feet away and watched: I marveled at the motion. His leaps seemed effortless; his steps flowed like water; his hand opened a pathway through which his arm, his shoulder, his torso, and his legs followed. As I watched, the music melted away and pure motion became a paintbrush. Air was his canvas; the painting vanished after each step, yielding straightaway to another. When the dance ended, I was left with a memory of the painting. Months later, the memory remains.

Nor is the memory about the dancer, but rather the dance. Yet the dance did not exist apart from the dancer, he and the motion were indistinguishable. He disappeared in the dance.

The single word for this description is "graceful." Yet such grace was anything but natural: this grace came as the result of years of discipline, practice, effort and sacrifice. The dancer, I'm sure, had fallen and suffered injury again and again. Certainly he had struggled with doubt, embarrassment, pain, fear, awkwardness, and discouragement. What emerged from the studio was a kind of resurrection, a resurrection of grace and beauty.

Grace grew from effort and focus. His motion inspired others. His art gave glory to God, and while it had the look of spontaneity it was anything but spur of the moment. Such grace grew from devotion: love of craft and creator.

I saw grace in motion, and my idea of grace deepened

and grew. What he had done in the natural, I began to desire in the Spirit. What does grace look like in everyday life? No dictionary can tell the tale; no theologian can describe the beauty: we must see it firsthand—but look sharp, this kind of grace disappears as quickly as it comes.

What if grace dances all around us? What do you suppose such gracefulness looks like in our relationships with others? And in what studio do we learn the dance of divine love?

The Grace of Discipline

The best lies always use a bit of the truth. That's certainly true of spiritual formation: after we understand the importance responding to God's grace, we might think God has done everything he's going to do. *"The rest is up to me,"* we think. *"I must meditate, pray, serve, study, contemplate, isolate, and even celebrate on my own. Jesus showed me how it's done. He died on the cross, paid the price, and now it's up to me."* And of course we *should* do these things, but that's where the lie takes hold: these activities are important not because of our effort, but because the Father is willing to do still more on our behalf.

Self-discipline has great power, but it comes at the risk of locating the source of that power in us instead of the grace of God. If will power alone brings spiritual growth, we have no need for his daily presence. The distinguishing mark between grace-empowerment and the pride of self discipline is that self-discipline says to others, "If I can do it, why can't you?"

James 4:6 reminds us: *"But he gives us more grace. That is why Scripture says: 'God opposes the proud but gives grace to the humble.'"* More grace. Greater grace. When we humble ourselves we position ourselves for greater grace. So it is with all the spiritual disciplines. His zealous love is the engine of his grace. He always wants to give more, because he loves so deeply. God's grace is the disciple's fuel for a supernatural life. Grace is the yellow sun; pride is kryptonite.

One sure indicator of a religiously closed mind is the

firm conviction that we have this Jesus thing figured out. We can handle it. The religiously closed mind is only interested in exporting its brand of spirituality, but it's impossible to drink in God's grace if we do nothing but tell others how to live their lives.

As mentors like Richard Foster and Dallas Willard have pointed out time and again, the spiritual disciplines are not hurdles to be cleared by the "serious" student of Jesus: the disciplines are practices that put us into position to receive more of his grace. The startling truth is that those who desire to live godly in Christ Jesus need *more* of God's grace than others who have no interest in spiritual transformation. Richard Foster sets us straight: "Grace is not a ticket to heaven, but the earth under our feet on the road with Christ."

The grace-empowered disciple realizes the daily need for God's presence. With that presence amazing things are possible. The Apostle Paul lived a disciplined and focused life during the years of ministry, but he was a force of super-nature, not nature. The grace-empowered disciple says, along with the Apostle Paul, *"By the grace of God I am what I am, and his grace to me was not without effect."* (1 Corinthians 15:10)

Our transformation is his work, accomplished as we present ourselves to "greater grace" again and again. If we limit his grace to the work of forgiveness, then forgiveness is all we will know. If we open ourselves up to his infinite grace then our destiny is the infinite God.

The Grace of Repentance

Silly stereotypes: they can get in the way. Even worse, they can hide the life-giving truth. For example, the beauties of the word *repent*.

See? Right away you saw the fire-and-brimstone, didn't you? Images of the grumpy preacher in *Footloose* and the irony of fundamentalists screaming "Repent!" while it's perfectly obvious what they really want is for you to burn in Hell forever. In the wrong mouth, "Repent!" is a hate-filled word. On the Jesus's lips, it's the kiss of life.

The Old Testament word is as simple as turning around: *you've taken a wrong turn, turn around and go back.* That's it. No accusation, no put-downs. When the Hebrews thought of repentance they thought in terms of getting back on track. C.S. Lewis makes repentance sound positively modern:

> *"Progress means getting nearer to the place you want to be. And if you have taken a wrong turning, then to go forward does not get you any nearer. If you are on the wrong road, progress means doing an about-turn and walking back to the right road; and in that case the man who turns back soonest is the most progressive man."*

The New Testament word repent is even better: *re-think. Get a new mind, change the way you process life.* It's the very first word of the Good News (Mark 1:15). The grace-filled gospel starts with "repent." John the Baptist and Jesus alike declared that a new reality

36

was breaking into the world; the Kingdom of God was at hand. The old ways of thinking and acting no longer applied. Think on that for a moment: "repent" is an offer of new life.

Ask anyone on the street if they would like to live a life free from regret. Astoundingly, amazingly, freedom from regret starts with this wonderful Kingdom call: repent! The scripture reveals the possibility of a life without regret. "*For the sorrow that is according to the will of God produces a repentance without regret, leading to salvation, but the sorrow of the world produces death.*" (II Corinthians 7: 10) Paul encourages his friends in Corinth to allow the Holy Spirit to breathe on such sorrow and allow it to be redeemed. This redemption starts with repentance, and leads to a life free from the burden of *what-ifs*.

Grace hides in the most unexpected places, but here's the secret: they are always the low places of life. Like water, like love, grace flows down, soaks in, and fosters new life. All these wonderful possibilities begin with the humility of repentance. It's not simply the way into God's Kingdom; it's the grace-filled way forward each day.

EXERCISE: MEANS OF GRACE

Richard Foster uses the phrase, *disciplined grace*. "It is *grace* because it is free; it is *disciplined* because there is something for us to do."

PRACTICE, PRACTICE, PRACTICE:

Be still. Invite the Holy Spirit to come near. Breathe.

Pray: "Spirit of God, would you please lead me into the greater means of grace?"

Read: Richard Foster's classic book, *Celebration of Discipline: The Path to Spiritual Growth* lays out a dozen practices that have led other believers into deep waters of God's grace. It may be worth exploring these paths.

Choose: Visit Foster' very useful website, *Renovaré*. (https://www.renovare.org/formation/practical-strategy). You'll find a list of these practices, along with ways to dive in. Why not pick one and dive in!

Do: Life in Christ is process of experiment and learning, that's why we speak of "spiritual practices" instead of spiritual goals. There's no pressure because Jesus has already done his part (and it was the impossible part). In turn, we live a lifetime of experimentation and joyful practice.

Grace at the Table

Surely Jesus believed that prostitutes were sinners, yet he welcomed them to his table. He ate and drank with them.

Surely Jesus understood that tax collectors betrayed their countrymen by helping the brutal Roman occupiers in his homeland, yet he welcomed tax collectors to his table as well.

Surely Jesus noticed how religious hypocrites and Pharisees misrepresented God's heart and laid heavy burdens on God's people, yet he dined with them and invited them to participate in his Father's kingdom.

Surely Jesus saw first-hand Peter's temper, James and John's foolish nationalism, even Judas' tortured and divided motivations, yet he broke bread with each one of them, sharing his very body and blood.

Jesus welcomed everyone to his table. He welcomed the clueless and the cruel. He engaged the outcast and the insider. He shared his life with his enemies because he came to turn enemies into family. His method was startling: he ate and drank with them. Wherever Jesus ate, it was his table. He turned water into wine and transformed ritual into everlasting love. No one was turned away.

He set an example for us to follow. At the cross, he did what only he could do. At the table, he demonstrated what we can do. The other day my wife and I tried to recall who had lived in our home during our 30+ years of marriage. We were surprised at even a partial list: a woman recovering from abortion; a married couple emerging from drug rehab; a fighter pilot far from home; the homeless; the working poor; international students; our immigrant neighbors; the lonely, the godless, the seekers. Sometimes the experience wasn't pleasant for us but each guest changed our understanding of grace, and nudged us further toward God's Kingdom. Welcoming the stranger to our table has always enriched us.

Jesus gave no one a pass on his or her rebellion or self-destructive ways. The sinless perfect representative of God's heart never lowered his standards or winked at injustice. Still, everyone was welcome around his table. He was no lightweight: if a moment called for brutal honestly, he fulfilled that need as well.

He did not negotiate, he fellowshipped. He refused to let disagreement separate him from others. Jesus possessed the proper opinions, the right positions, and perfect perspective, but never—not once—did he use his correct standing as a reason to alienate other people.

Perhaps we should remember to say grace over the people gathered around the table in addition to the food piled high on the table. Who is welcome at your table?

Jesus, Friend of Pharisees

A young girl named Mary told us what was coming. She sang a magnificent song that revealed Jesus would specialize in turning things topsy-turvy:

He has brought down rulers from their thrones
but has lifted up the humble.
He has filled the hungry with good things
but has sent the rich away empty. (Luke 1:52-53)

As we read the gospels, we see Mary's words played out again and again: Jesus shuts the mouths of the lawyers and scribes by asking them questions they cannot answer; Jesus lifts an adulterous woman up from the dust after her accusers have been silenced; Jesus intones *"Woe to you"* seven times toward those who think they have special insight into the ways of God.

Mary's song is true today as well. We love Jesus because he can stick it to the Man. He is the icon of the Father and iconoclast of the fat cats. We see in him an ancient model of our modern selves. Deep inside we know the Establishment types use religion to prop themselves up and keep the rest of us down. They are just gaming the system. This is the kick-ass Jesus who has finally exposed all the posers and fakes in the church, the Jesus who is even now leading the charge down the aisle, away from the altar, and out the red double-doors. We love the Jesus who has finally confirmed all our judgments about the hypocrites and losers who populate organized religion. Jesus the hipster is turning over the tables in God's house again. Finally, a Jesus who will tell those guys off!

Is it possible we've once again created him in our own image? Again. Mary's song is true today as well, but perhaps the roles have been reframed. In modern society we love to point out that Jesus ate with tax collectors and prostitutes. He crossed social boundaries. He was the friend of sinners. Sometimes we fail to note there is another group with whom he regularly dined: Pharisees.

And yet . . .

What if Jesus reclined with Pharisees for the very same reason he ate with the outcasts? What if he had the same mission whether he ate with Zacchaeus the taxman or with Simon the Pharisee? What if he cared for both? Perhaps the Lord knew we were all sick, all in need of a doctor.

Reading our rebellious ways into the ministry of Jesus is one of the dangers of our present age. We might assume he welcomed every sinner and condemned every priest. We might assume he ditched the synagogue for a day at the lake, or went to the Temple only to turn the tables. We might be surprised to discover that he loved his Father's house, or considered the Law as sweet as honey, or longed to hear the prophets read week after week.

The same man who welcomed Matthew the tax collector was also a friend to leaders and rich men like Nicodemus and Joseph of Arimathea. The same man who healed lepers and returned them to the community of Israel also had mercy on the daughter of a synagogue leader. The shepherd of Israel cared for the whole flock and fed all the sheep. Later, he went so far as to chase down Saul, that murderous "Pharisee of Pharisees" and drafted him into the Kingdom cause.

If we choose to follow the Master we must be prepared to follow him into any house. In his day the disciples were shocked because he crossed the threshold of a sinner's home. Perhaps today he shocks us by crossing the threshold of the church? Both houses stand in desperate need of his grace, and those who will carry such grace with them.

The Bible: God's Indispensible Grace Gift

Only fools and lawyers argue over the law, and both are highly trained specialists. The rest of us should leave such work to the experts. Sometimes they unite in their work, giving us silly civic ordinances prohibiting the transport of ice cream cones in your pocket, or whistling in public after 9:00PM, or banning birds from flying over historic statues. (No really: there are laws like that on the books of some American cities!)

I'd be content to leave the law to the fools and lawyers except for a troubling practice among religious people: they are in the habit of treating the Bible—especially the Old Testament—like a book of law. If there is anything worse than city ordinances against public singing before 8:00AM, it's when religious people turn the Bible into a book of laws.

It's understandable. The Old Testament sometimes calls itself "*the Law*" (Torah). Hebrew scholars, rabbis and Christian professors alike would like us to know *Torah* more properly means *instruction, teaching*, or even "*the way*." To continue to call the Old Testament "the Law" is an unfortunate translation, because life is more like a living room than a courtroom.

The Old Testament, that portion of the Bible we so often avoid, was the Bible that shaped Jesus's spiritual formation. Jesus was nourished on the stories of Adam, Enoch, Noah, Abraham, Isaac, Jacob, and Joseph—and that's just Genesis! Jesus chanted the *Shema*, memorized the ten words from Sinai, and paid close attention to the rituals of Leviticus. Jesus sang the Psalms, puzzled over the prophets, and marveled at the courage (and stupidity) of people portrayed in the Biblical narrative.

Jesus did not grow in wisdom and stature by memorizing the rules; he became a deep person by engaging the Old Testament with all his faculties: his mind, his heart, his imagination, his hopes, his questions, his fears, and his spirit. His Bible was all around him. He saw grass whither and fade, and then reflected on things that last forever; he saw the clumsy gait of an ox and then reflected the folly of following a prostitute to her house; when thunder answered the lightning, he heard the voice of God; he gleaned insight from industrious ants because the Proverbs had instructed him to go to the ants as part of his spiritual formation.

The sweetness of honey tasted to him of his Father's wisdom. In the poetry of Isaiah and Hosea the wisdom of God spoke to him through his parents' marriage; in the oil his mother used to cook; in the tramping of soldiers through his home town, and in the beauty of God's mercy each new sunrise: Jesus did not need some someone to bring the Bible alive, his world was alive with the Bible. He understood at a gut level that God's word was living and active, and that everyday life teemed with the deep truth of the word of God.

Meanwhile, in our modern age, we think "Bible study" is the stuff of ancient languages and word origins. Like either lawyers or fools (you decide) we ponder over the meaning and application of cross-cultural studies or socio-psychological interpretations. We think Bible study is more like hard work and not at all like a feast. We march with grim determination through our "quiet times," secretly wondering who will make the sacred text as least as engaging as late night TV.

The Bible—both Old and New Testaments—is the Father's indispensible grace-gift to followers of Jesus. With just a bit more grace we can discover that the written word on the page will bring us to the Living Word of life.

Goodness, Glory, and Grace

Do you have trouble finding grace in the pages of the Old Testament? In the middle of betrayal and spiritual adultery on the part of the children of Israel, God chose to demonstrate his goodness to Moses. Exodus 33:12-23 tells the story of the time the people of Israel—freshly recused from slavery in Egypt—crafted a golden calf and worshipped the statue as "the god who brought us out of Egypt."

Moses wanted to give up on leading God's people, and give up on life. Can you blame him? Some days are diamonds, some days are stones, and some days are calf manure. Inside this very strange story (and it takes only a moment to read) we can find life-changing grace:

1). As Moses pleads with God for help, God answers simply, *"My Presence will go with you, and I will give you rest."* God's first answer is to offer his presence. It's what we need most. We can never conjure up his presence; it is always a grace-gift.

2). Moses responds with wisdom that still applies for us today: *"What else will distinguish me and your people from all the other people on the face of the earth?"* The distinguishing mark of God's people is his presence. In times of victory or trouble, his presence is our identity. It's an identity only grace can give.

3). This kindness from God emboldens Moses to push all the chips into the middle of the table, *"Show me your glory,"* Moses asks. What a strange request when

50

there are so many problems to solve! Grace teaches us that our deepest need is not a solution to our immediate problems, but the abiding glory of his presence.

4). Finally, even as God himself says yes to Moses, God offers a gentle instruction. Moses asked, *"Show me your glory,"* and God says, *"I will cause my goodness to pass in front of you."* From this we learn one of the ways God demonstrates his *glory* is to show us his *goodness.*

These four observations show a pathway to discovering grace: why not ask him today to open your eyes to his goodness?

Now, I must confess: I've fallen asleep at my desk twice this morning as I've researched this section of the book. I've been reading entries in theological dictionaries and books on systematic theology, trying to see if anyone understands the word *Glory.*

John, at the very beginning of his gospel, makes a direct connection between glory and grace: *"We have seen his glory, the glory of the one and only Son, who came from the Father, full of grace and truth."* As he looked intently at the grace and truth about Jesus, John couldn't get away from what he saw: he used the word *glory* 19 times in his gospel, more than all three of the other gospels combined. Glory is the kind of word us moderns have lost completely. If we rediscover God's glory we will also recover a greater understanding of his grace.

Glory is a strange word these days. It has the feel of movies like *Gladiator,* or the hyped opening of a Super Bowl. Religious people use it, too, but I'm not sure we know what it's all about. It conjures up notions of Pentecostals run amuck shouting, "Glory Hallelujah!"

What if the glory of God isn't the stuff of Old Testament stories, Hollywood hoopla, or religious delusions? What if glory is a substance so real it burns our skin, or kills cancer better than chemo? What if God designed his glory to be an agent of change? What if it's really true that the glory of Jesus is "filled with grace and truth?" The Apostle Paul thought so: *"But we all, with unveiled face, beholding as in a mirror the glory of the Lord, are being transformed into the same image from glory to glory, just as from the Lord, the Spirit."* (2 Corinthians 3:18)

Another what if. What if, in quoting Romans 3:23 we focused on our destiny instead of our sin? The famous verse reminds us *"all have sinned and fall short of the glory of God."* We have walked the Romans road so often we think only of our shortcomings but not the goal: we were made to live in his glory and reflect that glory. It was game-changer for me. True story: as a 19 year-old I experienced the glory of God in an arena of 3,000 pastors. A shining cloud of God's glory manifested in the arena: our order of service halted, we removed our shoes, and grown men wept. That one encounter changed my life forever. Years later I learned my wife had a similar experience in the setting of a house church, and the effect was the same: she knew she belonged to Jesus forever.

God's grace destines us to progress from glory to glory. What would it mean in real life if our expectations were focused on this infinite path, a path designed to transform us more and more into his image? How would it change things if we awoke to our destiny to be conformed to the image of Christ?

One of the unspoken needs of the western church is to rediscover the stuff of Biblical legend, called glory. We, too, should ask (as Moses did), "*Show me your glory!*" Someone *has* seen that day. Jesus spoke of it when he said he saw the sons and daughters of the kingdom shining like the sun, but we thought he was just being poetic. He was actually showing us the full extent of God's grace.

Grace Teaches

The more I read the New Testament, the more all-encompassing grace becomes. Instead of presenting grace as a repeatable sin-cleansing bargain, the Bible presents a grace that continues to reach into our lives day after day in more ways than we expect. The Apostle Paul, under the inspiration of the Holy Spirit, wrote to a young pastor:

> *The grace of God that brings salvation has appeared to all men. It teaches us to say "No" to ungodliness and worldly passions, and to live self-controlled, upright and godly lives in this present age, while we wait for the blessed hope - the glorious appearing of our great God and Savior, Jesus Christ, who gave himself for us to redeem us from all wickedness and to purify for himself a people that are his very own, eager to do what is good.* (Titus 2:11–14).

Many believers have never heard these verses declared from the pulpit. Grace appears in the passage with phrases like *"self-controlled'* or *"upright and godly lives."* What kind of grace is this? If grace means getting off scot-free, why is grace teaching us a new way to live?

Most believers are very familiar with *"the grace that brings salvation,"* but not many churchgoers have ever heard of a grace that *"teaches us to say No to ungodliness and worldly passions, and to live self-controlled, upright and godly lives in this present age."*

Most believers are familiar with a saving grace capable of securing heaven after we die, but have never considered the possibility that God's grace can nurture us in this present age.

Why would grace leave us naked and bleeding on the side of the road? Would grace allow sin to rule over us all the days of our lives? Apparently God's grace is after more than wiping the slate clean week after week. The grace of God wants to teach us a new way to live.

If grace is the teacher, we are the students, and all of life is the classroom. If we possess the humility to become learners, God's grace not only transports us to heaven when we die, it brings heaven close to us while we live.

Ours to Give

The Apostle Paul opened every letter with the words "grace and peace." Some people might think these words are a formality, but these words—even if they were formalities—were breathed out by the Holy Spirit. In the New Testament epistles, even the greetings are part of the inspired scripture!

I believe Paul gave each congregation grace and peace because they were his to give. Jesus had instructed the original twelve: *"Whatever house you enter, let your first words be, 'peace to this house.'"* (Luke 10:5) Jesus had in mind something more than words, because he observed that a greeting of peace could rest upon the people in that house, or return to the one that gave the greeting. This peace Jesus instructed the disciples to give was something real, something tangible, no less tangible than handing someone a loaf of bread. Decades later, Paul, a follower of Jesus, wrote to the churches of God scattered across the Roman world, and his first words are *"grace and peace."*

Paul himself possessed grace and peace. He apparently had a surplus: he could give it away. In many cases Paul was the founder of the church to which he wrote. He wrote to encourage what was good in these churches and to offer correction for whatever needed help: how often do we look upon correction and teaching as sources of the peace and grace of God? For those who have given it any thought at all, God's grace and peace should be prized above almost anything else in our lives. Many of Paul's churches faced persecution from the outside, some experienced disagreements on the inside. All of them needed grace and peace. They were so important that Paul presented these gifts up front, just as a guest would before entering a house.

Paul wanted his friends to experience God's grace and peace, and when necessary he brought powerful words of reproof. From our perspective twenty centuries later we understand that each letter was the word of God— then and now. Those people who first heard the words of Paul read aloud in the congregation had a choice: they could listen beyond the mere words of the letter and in so doing receive the grace and peace offered them, or, like the householder in Luke 10 refuse to receive the grace of God and the peace of God as it appeared to them.

How often does God's grace or peace appear to us in some form we may not recognize? Do we receive the words of loved ones as God's grace in our lives? Do we ever consider the instruction we receive from those in authority has the potential to bring God's peace?

Nor were Paul's words only about receiving: his greetings were examples of what we have to give. Have we received some measure of grace? Of peace? Jesus had straightforward instructions to his followers: *"freely you've received, therefore freely give."* If we have received any grace from God then we have garce to give. Don't worry, you won't run out! Paul's famous words from Romans 8:1, *"Therefore, there is now no condemnation for those who are in Christ Jesus,"* were not words he claimed exclusively for himself. He was speaking them over those who were listening to his letter. Many believers have quoted this verse on their own behalf in order to fight off guilt and condemnation. Have we ever quoted them on behalf of others?

If God has given us peace in any area of our lives, we can give that peace as well. One disciple may have learned the secret of contentment with respect to financial matters. Another may have learned how to place everyday fears at the feet of Jesus. Do we ever consider that the peace we've received in our walk with God might be the very thing we can teach others? He blesses us so that we can be a blessing to others.

Our everyday lives are no different than the times in which Paul wrote his letters. Words grace and peace are not mere formalities, they are ours to give.

God's Gracious Voice

God does some of his best work at sunrise, and he never says a word about it. Each morning the heavens declare the glory of God without the benefit of advertising, hype, or self-promotion.

The heavens declare the glory of God;
*   the skies proclaim the work of his hands.*
Day after day they pour forth speech;
*   night after night they display knowledge.*
There is no speech or language
*   where their voice is not heard.*
Their voice goes out into all the earth,
*   their words to the ends of the world.*
*   In the heavens he has pitched a tent for the sun,*
which is like a bridegroom coming forth from his
pavilion,
*   like a champion rejoicing to run his course.*
It rises at one end of the heavens
*   and makes its circuit to the other;*
*   nothing is hidden from its heat. (Psalm 19:1-6)*

There are those who say, "Good morning, Lord!" while others say, "Good Lord, it's morning!" His mercies are available to both groups, but only one will see his glory.

Daybreak is only one example: spectacular and quiet. Like resurrection. We are reminded each day that God delights in new possibilities. Each morning the message

60

comes again: because of his great love we are not consumed, his mercies are new every morning.

Dawn differs from daybreak, and his voice speaks again: the transition from night to day is subtle. It's slow. Dawn is process, not an event. The hope of transformation is displayed each day, reminding us that coming alive in Jesus Christ is not like flipping a light switch, but rather like the coming of the sun. "*The path of the righteous is like the first gleam of dawn, shining ever brighter till the full light of day.*" (Proverbs 4:18)

Nor does he stop speaking just because the day is begun. King David saw the sun trace across the sky, felt its warmth on his face, and heard the voice of God. God's voice engages all the senses. By his light we not only see, we can actually feel the warmth of his love. It can grow into a blaze of glory.

Once we come alive to the sound of his voice in the earth, we discover it everywhere. One of my friends heard the sound of the Spirit as he planted flowers. He stopped for just a moment, felt the breeze on his neck and heard its sound in the leaves. To be aware of the breeze is to be aware of his presence. It's a matter of training ourselves to take notice.

The voice of God is available to everyone. The heavens encircle the earth. All of humankind is included. Each of us can see his works. Rich and poor alike can see the sunrise or sunset. Rich and poor alike can ignore the majesty as well. The heavens encircle the earth, enabling people of every tribe and tongue to discover his goodness. He speaks without language to the hearts of men. Children are attuned to the wonder, but the busy-ness of adults drowns the still small voice.

Nor does he speak only in the day. Once my ear became attuned to his voice I found myself worshipping God under the night sky. I heard the silent speech of the stars. The still of the night is vibrant with his presence.

There's a difference between God's greatness and his love. Some people are impressed by God's power and might, the wise fall down in worship at the realization of his love. The sight of a single star in the evening is enough to provoke awe at God's greatness. A sky filled with stars declares his unfailing love.

Grace like Manna

The steadfast love of the Lord never ceases; his mercies never come to an end; they are new every morning; great is your faithfulness. ~ Lamentations 3:22-23

Is there anything quite like the aroma of baking bread? Without overpowering the house it permeates the air with an invitation to come and eat. If you were lucky enough to grow up in a home that celebrates each morning with fresh biscuits, you woke up to the scent of goodness in the morning.

Perhaps because I've never met a carbohydrate I didn't like, or perhaps because God served fresh biscuits to the people of Israel in the desert wilderness every morning for forty years, I've come to expect the smell of his goodness every morning. I've begun to train myself to discover his lovingkindness day by day.

Consider the book of Lamentations: hidden midway through these suffering poems is the revelation of God's constant and faithful provision for each one of us. In part, the lesson of these verses calls us to look for his mercies daily, to sniff them out, because regardless of our circumstances he is present and overflowing with mercy. If the weeping poet of Lamentations became convinced of God's daily mercies can we not discover the same?

We were made to eat fresh bread. We do not have to live off of aging mercy and stale grace. Who would be satisfied to eat biscuits three days old, or bread frozen and served a month later? No. The Heavenly Father is a better parent than that. Amazingly, the poet of Lamentations suggested that even when life is at its most difficult stages, we can be assured of God's constant and daily care.

What if we determined to discover the reality of this revelation? What if each day was a hunt to discover the mercies which he prepared this morning? What if this is not simply a good idea, but the grace to restore our senses, heal our eyes, and enable us to taste his goodness? What if we engaged in the discipline of searching out and identifying his fresh mercy? If we choose, it can move us to daily action, to search for—and discover—the gifts he has placed in our path.

New morning, new mercies: where will you discover the table he has set today?

EXERCISE: STEWARDS OF GRACE

The Apostle Peter calls us *stewards of grace* (1 Peter 4:10). We are the caretakers of God's grace.

TAKE TEN MINUTES:

Be still. Invite the Holy Spirit to come near. Breathe.

Review: Mark 6:33-44 reports one occasion when Jesus fed five thousand people. Take a few minutes to revisit that account. Read it over once, or even twice.

Imagine: After reviewing the story, try to put yourself *into* the story by imagining you are one of his disciples. (You *are* one, aren't you?) In this story the disciples are the stewards of God's grace.

Be Specific: How did you feel when Jesus told *you* to "give them something to eat"? What did the boy with the loaves and fish look like? How did Jesus bless the food? What did your basket look like as you began to distribute the food? How did it feel to see the miracle of multiplication again and again?

Do: Can you imagine playing the same role in modern life? What would it look like to distribute God's grace?

TAKE TEN YEARS:

Your imagination can change the way you read the scripture. Stewarding God's grace can change your life.

Getting in on Heaven's Joke

When comedian Steve Martin was trying to break into the big time, he refused to compromise his groundbreaking brand of comedy. His attitude was, *"this is funny, you just haven't gotten it yet."* God's sense of humor is the same: just stick around long enough and you, too, will laugh with all of heaven.

> *As evening approached, the disciples came to him and said, "This is a remote place, and it's already getting late. Send the crowds away, so they can go to the villages and buy themselves some food."*
>
> *Jesus replied, "They do not need to go away. You give them something to eat.""We have here only five loaves of bread and two fish," they answered.*
>
> *"Bring them here to me," he said. And he directed the people to sit down on the grass. Taking the five loaves and the two fish and looking up to heaven, he gave thanks and broke the loaves. Then he gave them to the disciples, and the disciples gave them to the people. They all ate and were satisfied, and the disciples picked up twelve basketfuls of broken pieces that were left over. The number of those who ate was about five thousand men, besides women and children. (Matthew 14:15-21)*

When the disciples were faced with a crowd-control problem and had no resources, Jesus suggested the answer was to invite everyone to dinner. It's hilarious. Before the evening was over, we are treated to the sight of each disciple lugging away a basketful of extra food. The joke was on them. They told the Lord, "*Let everyone fend for themselves,*" but Jesus knew that the path to abundance was caring for others.

Heaven rings with the laughter of paradox. Five plus two equals twelve baskets full. God plus you equals infinity. That day on the Galilean hillside Jesus had an object lesson for his friends. He could have lectured, but instead he invited his closest followers to participate in the crazy math of God's Kingdom.

School is in session for us, if we so choose:

"You give them something to eat." Jesus demonstrated that ministry calls us to take responsibility for those who respond. When the workday was over, the disciples were ready to pack it in. Jesus invited his disciples to set a larger table, even if it seems ridiculous.

"We have here only . . . " The disciples looked at the "only," Jesus looked at the bread and fish. The students saw their lack; the Master saw the possibilities. In the Kingdom of God we are asked to learn a new kind of math, the kind that starts with recognizing what is, not what is not.

"He gave thanks . . ." Yes, I know, this is a commonplace observation. Everyone who studies this event notes that Jesus gave thanks. But the commonplace can become easy to

ignore. Jesus demonstrated thanks-giving time and again. It was the Master's habit. To become like Jesus is to live in mindset of perpetual thanks.

"He broke the loaves . . ." Too often, even in our thankfulness, we want to hold on to what we have. When Jesus broke the bread he demonstrated that whatever we have should be—must be—broken and shared. Even more amazing is the lesson that brokenness is God's means of provision. When we hold back, others go hungry.

"He gave . . . and the disciples gave." Here is where the miracle happened, and how the miracle happened is instructive. Jesus included his disciples in the miraculous. What he gave to them was multiplied in their hands as they gave it to others. How often do we hold on to what the Lord gives us? We are provided for, but we miss the miracle by keeping it to ourselves. Jesus laid down this ministry principle time and again: *"Freely you've received, therefore freely give."* (Matthew 10:8)

"The disciples picked up twelve baskets full." On the back end of this supernatural meal was an abundant provision for each follower of Jesus. Because they tended to the needs of others, they themselves ended up with more food than they needed. Do we want abundant provision? The Lord recommends looking after the needs of others.

The laughter of heaven pours forth when we discover that it's the Father's joy to give, and give again. Some churches join in the laughter by randomly giving away gift cards to shoppers in the grocery store: you should see the look on people's faces when a stranger pays the bill!

This is grace: he wants us to be in on the joke. He invites us to confound the wisdom of the wise and the planning of the careful with hilarious generosity. It's his idea of a good time. It can become ours as well.

EGR: Extra Grace Required

My friend tells the story of a pastor who had a certain way with difficult people. You know: the kind of people who are whiny, needy, angry, insecure, volatile, vain, messy, picky, overbearing, ugly, no-fun, un-hip, clueless, or otherwise not-with-the-program. This pastor asked his staff to be patient with such people, and referred to these unfortunates as *EGR*: Extra Grace Required. The difficult people in the church needed extra grace.

Huh.

The phrase *Extra Grace Required* stuck with me for days. I began to wonder: how much is the regular amount of grace? Is there a grace manual somewhere that details the proper amount of grace for each person? What about people afflicted with multiple shortcomings? (I qualify for several conditions listed above—but I'm not going to tell you which ones.)

(OK, it's all of them.)

So here's the first problem: the well-meaning pastor implies that grace is a tool in the pastoral tool-kit. Reach into ministerial bag and grab some ointment labeled *ERG*. Apply generously, as if grace is something dispensed from the *Haves* and given nobly to the *Have-nots*. As if grace is drug, and the minister is the pharmacist. But grace isn't a salve to be applied; it's a feast to be shared. We welcome others to the very table we enjoy, where together we revel in God's bounty.

God gives grace. We share it.

Second: I imagine this pastor (yes, the one I never met, the one my friend told me about, the one I have turned into the object of my own creation) has read Ephesians 4:7, *"But grace was given to each one of us according to the measure of Christ's gift"*, and decided that grace comes prepackaged from Heaven: small, medium, large, and EGR. Yet I pause at the phrase *according to the measure of Christ's gift* and wonder how we measure the Lord's gift—or even what that gift is, precisely. I wonder what size gift comes from an infinite God.

Finally, this pastor had it backwards: difficult people do not require extra grace, I do. The problem is not their requirement: it is my lack. When the depth of human need is beyond the limits of my patience and empathy, when the hurt and fear goes deeper than my ability to counsel it away, when I reach the boundaries of my Christlikeness, *I am the one* that needs the fuel of grace. I am the one who needs grace to listen to others without the urge to move on to the next patient. I am the one who needs to see Jesus in the face of each difficult, hurting person. I am the one who requires not "extra" grace, but the real thing, the true supernatural substance from Heaven: the grace of God. Ministry based upon my own resources will produce disciples that look like me, and that fearsome thought should be reason enough to cry out for grace to sustain me.

Extra Grace Required? Well, yes: for me.

Grace & Judgment

I once forgave a man for being an ass, but he was offended by my mercy. It turns out mercy cuts like a knife. Mercy triumphs over judgment, but is it not also true that without judgment mercy cannot exist?

The same truth, softer: in Narnia, Aslan the Christ-figure lion bounds into the scene and sets things right. Most of us love the story with a too-convenient love. We love Narnia because we do not live in Narnia. But consider Edmund, the traitor/king: for him Narnia was no walk in the park. Edmund met the hard truth of his own resentment toward his brother and his willingness to betray his family for a mess of Turkish Delight.

In Narnia large issues are at stake: The creatures of the realm long for Aslan's appearing. Says Mr. Beaver: "*Wrong will be right when Aslan is in sight, at the sound of his roar, sorrows will be no more. When he bares his teeth, winter meets its death, when he shakes his mane we shall know spring again.*" Yet neither *sorrow* nor *winter* happened by chance. The Lion brought judgment to realm, and those who had chosen poorly were brought face-to-face with their choices—and how their choices impacted others.

My asinine friend protested, "Maybe I am a bit blunt, but who are you to say so?" He resented the judgment in the message even though it contained was mercy and grace. Perhaps, too, he did not care for the messenger.

That great man after God's own heart, King David,

cries out, *"Search me, Oh God, and know my heart . . . See if there is any wicked way in me."* This is a pious prayer. Equally important is how God answers this prayer: who will deliver the results of God's search? In David's case it was Nathan the prophet. Nathan's words were difficult for David to hear.

We prefer justice at a distance and cannot abide it too close to home. Justice at a distance is the easy work of loving the brother we cannot see, while we avoid the reality of our actions toward our neighbor. We can easily identify the far-away wrong in others while running from the close-to-home wrong in ourselves. Justice at a distance is comfortable because we need not examine ourselves. It allows us to be on the right side of the equation every time. I find myself loving Justice as an ideal, but hiding from the judgments over my own life.

The formula *Justice, good/judgment, bad* is alchemy. It causes me to believe things may be set right without the hard work of seeing something is wrong. The chilling truth is in a world with no wrongs, all manner of evil thrives. Do I really want to create a home-environment where evil can thrive *in me?*

Jesus spoke to us with a liberating genius: *"It is not the healthy who need a doctor, but the sick. But go and learn what this means: 'I desire mercy, not sacrifice.' For I have not come to call the righteous, but sinners."*

Perhaps this is why Peter suggests, *"It is time for judgment to begin in God's household."* We need not be afraid of this kind of judgment for one shining reason: this judgment points to mercy and grace, which

75

lead to freedom. "*Who will bring any charge against those whom God has chosen?*' asked Paul. "*It is God who justifies. Who then is the one who condemns? No one. Christ Jesus who died—more than that, who was raised to life—is at the right hand of God and is also interceding for us.*"

Here is the good news: the only true source of judgment is the very one who has demonstrated he will pay any price to set us right. Will we welcome such severe grace and mercy in our lives? It's the path to a life beyond mere forgiveness, into the freedom of grace.

Learning From Our Sin

Here's the pattern: I choose sin, which is bad enough. Worse still—afterward—a voice in my head tries to drag me deeper still. It's the voice of the Adversary: he whispers enticement before my sin and shouts condemnation after. His is a voice skilled in subtle influence followed by paralyzing guilt. It's a voice filled with accusation. He is a liar and the father of lies; lies are his native tongue.

But even in the wreck of my God-awful choices there is another voice. After my sin comes another still, small voice. It sounds like a storytelling prophet trying to open the eyes of a privileged king. "Return to me," it whispers, "and I will return to you." It is the voice of Jesus asking Peter, "Do you love me?"

Sin brings death, but Jesus is no mere medical examiner doing a post-mortem. He raises the victim to life.

This is the glory of God: he speaks to us even in our sin. The Great Alchemist turns our sin into the stuff of restoration. His message is restoration, and what's more, he takes our defeat and turns it into the very fabric of instruction. Have you ever learned from your sin? This is grace: God is not only ready to forgive; he is eager to teach. If we are open to God's voice, even our sin become grace in his hands. He will show us the path and correct our steps, not by insisting on obedience but by revealing our hearts. Not by counting ours sins against us, but by teaching us a new way to live.

After I choose anger, Jesus wants to reveal its source, and heal the weakness that led to sin. After I choose greed, Jesus wants to reveal my insecurity, and heal the weakness that led to sin. After I choose lust, Jesus wants to reveal my desire, and heal the weakness that led to sin. After I choose judgment, Jesus wants to reveal my pride, and heal the weakness that led to sin. (Do you get the idea that God wants to heal the weaknesses that lead to sin?)

Jesus is not the kind of person who simply says, "Go, and sin no more." He also makes his command possible. What he asks, he empowers. He takes us to the source and gives us hope. Resurrection isn't just for Jesus; it's for us. It's not just for the end of days, it's so we can walk in newness of life. Sin puts us in the tomb; Jesus rolls away the stone—as often as we need.

Untimely, Unlikely Grace

Jesus, fresh from the grave, revealed himself to quite a list of people. In fact, we have the actual list: *"He was raised on the third day according to the Scriptures, and He appeared to Cephas, then to the twelve. After that He appeared to more than five hundred brethren at one time, most of whom remain until now, but some have fallen asleep; then He appeared to James, then to all the apostles; and last of all, as to one untimely born, He appeared to me also."* (1 Corinthians 15:4-8) Notice the list-maker puts himself at the end of the parade, as he should. He knew he didn't belong. A preschooler playing *"One-of-these-things-is-not-like-the-others"* would've removed Paul from the list in a heartbeat. The Apostle Paul, last of all: one untimely born.

Paul didn't walk with Jesus on the roads of Galilee or hear the Sermon on the Mount firsthand. Years later, in the most untimely way, Jesus appeared to Paul, roughed him up on the highway, and left him blind in a foreign town. Yet when he was healed something more than scales fell from his eyes: he saw God's grace as both comfort and provocation.

Grace sees things for what they are: Paul understood he was not fit to be called an apostle. He persecuted the church of God. Paul himself points to his violent, murderous heart, but not like one asking for parole—he was a man pardoned. But divine pardon does not change the facts. Paul says simply, *"by the grace of God I am what I am, and His grace toward me did not prove vain."* He is strangely content with his past. Grace doesn't whitewash history: it builds on the ugly facts and makes them the foundation for a glory unimagined. The one untimely born became the herald of transformation.

Paul would be the first to tells us, though, that contentment is only half of gracework: "*but I labored even more than all of them, yet not I, but the grace of God with me.*" The very grace capable of bringing contentment fuels the work of the herald. As plainly as Paul would tell you he is the least of the Apostles, he also looks you in the eye and lays claim to being the strongest hand in the field.

Both are grace: "*I am what I am*" and "*I labored even more.*" Grace lives between contentment and hard work, entirely at home with either neighbor. The pardon becomes fuel for the task.

Jesus Used Grace

If you want to know what the full potential for your life can be, look at Jesus. All that he did during his earthly ministry was done through reliance on the Holy Spirit. That means by grace, we can follow his example.

Have you ever considered the possibility that Jesus himself depended upon the grace of God?

Our modern, limited view of grace is directly attributable to the separation we see between Jesus and us. We have been schooled regarding his divinity but the lessons stop with respect to his humanity. Without putting it into so many words, we see Jesus cruising through the challenges of everyday life with the ease of walking on water.

Perhaps we are able to recognize the human side of Jesus in the garden of Gethsemane, where he cries out in anguish because of the task ahead. We understand the fear of suffering and the desire to avoid it. We understand why Jesus would say, "*Father take this cup from me . . .* " but we have no idea how the grace of God helped Jesus to develop into the kind of person who could also say, " *. . . yet not my will, but yours be done.*"If our view of God's grace is limited to receiving forgiveness, Jesus cannot be our model for how to receive grace, live in grace, and depend upon grace. Who taught Peter, John, Paul and countless other believers how to live the kind of grace-filled life we see in Acts and the history of the church? How does grace apply to everyday life in a manner that we are conscious of the supply and know how to use it?

If the grace of God is shortened to mean only forgiveness, we are forever trapped in a cycle of sin and grace and more sin again. Where do we see that cycle in the life of Jesus? We cannot see it because it is not there. What is there for us to see is grace in operation when Jesus was tempted in the wilderness, when he wept at the tomb of Lazarus, even when he angrily drove the merchants from the Temple. He is our model for the operation of grace in times of testing, in sorrow, and in every human emotion we face. He said "No" to ungodliness and worldly passions, and lived a self-controlled, upright and godly life in this present age. He can be the author of such grace toward us, because what he has received he freely shares.

The Private Side of Grace

The Father communicates his grace in ways both big and small. When you're on the interstate, doing 85, you need a big sign: white reflective letters two feet high against a green background, shouting "Exit Here."

Late at night, when your baby is sick, you're looking for a much smaller sign, in print so small you reach for your glasses and turn on the light, *"Ages 2-4, one teaspoon every four hours, do not exceed four doses in 24 hours."* You read the label twice to make sure you've got it right. Both sets of words communicate God's grace.

It's easy to see the public side of grace: it's represented in the cross. The cross is splashed across church buildings like so many interstate signs, signaling that the love of God is available to any who will exit here. The news is so good it deserves an elevated platform. But those who see grace written large on the landscape might think that's all there is. Still, grace has a private side as well. Consider some of the private sides of God's grace:

§ There's a kind of grace you can't see from the highway: "Grace saves us from life without God," says Richard Foster. "Even more it empowers us for life *with* God." The grace we receive at the new birth is only the introduction. Students of Jesus need grace for growth as well. Grace opens up the startling possibility that we do not have to yo-yo between sin and forgiveness, sin and

84

forgiveness. It becomes possible to yield every choice, every thought to God, because his grace can teach us to say "no" to ungodliness (Titus 2:11-12).

§ Three times the scripture reminds us *"God resists the proud, but gives grace to the humble."* Humility is part of the private side of grace. When the Father sees one of his children willing to take the low place in the family, he pours out an extra portion of grace to provide strength for service to others. Humility draws the blessing and favor of God. The same one who stripped to the waist and washed our feet rejoices when we learn to prefer one another. Think of George Bailey in *It's A Wonderful Life.* George, the older brother, stays behind in Bedford Falls so his younger brother can leave town in order to go to college. But quietly, over the years, George grows in his love for the town, and becomes a type of savior, rescuing Bedford Falls from the greed of others.

§ Dallas Willard's famous phrase, *"grace is not opposed to effort, it is opposed to earning"* reminds us of the proper response to God's saving work. The Apostle Paul understood the private side of grace as well. The "famous" apostle is the same one who described his task as one of *"great endurance; in troubles, hardships and distresses; in beatings, imprisonments and riots; in hard work, sleepless nights and hunger,"* (2 Corinthians 6:5) all in order to share what he himself had been given. Paul had no trouble seeing the connection between grace and effort.

§ **Paul was so convinced of our ongoing need for grace** that he opened every letter he wrote (every one!) with the greeting, "grace to you, and peace." Perhaps—just perhaps—the Holy Spirit and Paul considered grace and peace indispensable to everyday Christian life.

What is the private side of grace? The private side of grace is the discovery that the new birth should be followed by growth into the image of Jesus. The private side of grace is when we begin to take on the family likeness. It begins when his children are old enough to understand that the Father sees what is done in secret-- not in order to catch us in transgression, but to reward those hearts that joyfully follow his example.

Defining Grace

Beware the questions of a child. The other day our fourth-grader asked, "So what is grace, exactly?" It only took a moment for me to discover "*Grace*" doesn't yield an exact definition.

When I tried to simplify it to "God's goodness toward us," she asked, "Then why don't we just say '*goodness*?'" When I tried the legal angle her eyes clouded over. I realized I could kill the word if I kept going so I gave up the legal track.

"Why do people say that ballerinas are 'graceful'?" she asked. (Great: I have a ten year-old philologist on my hands.) We talked for a half-hour, which is like graduate-level work for someone her age. We could've looked up more than 15 dictionary entries for the simple five-letter word, or another five-to-ten idioms ranging from "fall from grace" to "*coup de grace*," and we draw no closer to our goal.

This is the wonder of Grace: as big as the sky, as close as your next breath. Grace is insubstantial and ethereal—nothing more than an idea—an idea that continues to change the world. Grace is love made practical. Grace empowers. Grace cares not for the argument, but for the people arguing. Grace has an agenda beyond the truth. Grace knows that the frustrated heart would rather sit on the sidelines and be wrong than be forced to run with the schoolyard bullies who are right. Grace turns its nose up at winning the fight and aims instead to win the person. Grace plays the long game.

The only unsatisfying part of God's grace is it's too big to comprehend. Would we want it any other way?

Unmerited Favor

This is the first definition of grace I learned years ago: *grace is God's unmerited favor.* My well-meaning instructors taught me (and it's true) that there is nothing I can do to earn God's favor. God chooses to forgive simply because of his mercy and the sacrifice of his son, Jesus. We didn't earn it, and we can never earn his forgiveness, his love, or his favor.

God's unmerited favor is a perfectly good phrase—but the words don't tell the whole story: our application of the words matter as much as their meaning. Too often we live our lives with the emphasis on *unmerited* while ignoring the word *favor,* as if the Father has forgiven us, but he's not very happy about it. Frequently we project our difficulties on to God. Because grace and forgiveness are difficult for us, it's an easy step to believe that the Father is unhappy about them, too. But it's his joy to give grace. It's his delight. When God gives grace he is acting out of his nature, his very being. How can we receive the full measure of his grace if we are convinced it comes from a grumpy God?

How we receive his grace is important for another reason: the secret for us to *give* grace freely is to become conformed to his joyful, grace-giving nature. Giving grace to others becomes a joy when we ourselves become like our Lord. Can we imagine the possibility of a life where giving grace to others is not only life-giving to them but also for us as well?

When we emphasize the *unmerited* side of this

definition we remind ourselves constantly of our failure instead of his goodness. Which atmosphere promotes spiritual health, living in the mud of our own inadequacies or in the cleansing water of his grace?

Unmerited *favor.* Bible teacher Derek Prince has provided the best description of *favor* I've ever encountered: "The humble child and servant of God who walks in the fear of the Lord under the cloud of God's favor is a 'rain-bringer.' He automatically blesses everybody he comes in contact with. There is a fragrance about him, a presence within him—something overshadowing him that goes everywhere he goes." I want to be the kind of person who brings the fragrance of God's favor—his grace—to everyone I meet. As the Apostle Paul described his own ministry, *"We are to God the pleasing aroma of Christ among those who are being saved and those who are perishing."* (2 Corinthians 2:15)

Who Will Cover Me?

I've decided to do a bit of griping today—but only for one paragraph. Be warned. Here it comes.

Social media is filled with criticism, finger pointing and name-calling between family members. Recently a famous Christian minister said something stupid (and it *was* stupid) and before you could say "trending topic" he was pummeled by criticism from others within the faith. Or: someone is hurt by their mistreatment at a local church, so they adopt Lone Ranger status and start a new blog about how the "real" church has nothing to do with organized religion. Or: one faction of believers promotes an opinion and, in response, another faction labels them heretical or dangerous. It's *Jersey Shore* for believers, only uglier.

There. I vented for one paragraph. But (no surprise) I don't feel any better, nor have I changed anyone's opinion or behavior. We remain the same.

There's a more excellent way. "*The end of all things is near. Therefore be alert and of sober mind so that you may pray. Above all, love each other deeply, because love covers over a multitude of sins. Offer hospitality to one another without grumbling. Each of you should use whatever gift you have received to serve others, as faithful stewards of God's grace in its various forms.*" (1 Peter 4:7-10)

One phrase shines through the layers of meaning in Peter's words: "*love covers over a multitude of sins.*" He is talking about a community of people who received the great treasure of God's grace and asked to steward that treasure by how they treat one another. This stewardship includes the kind of love capable of protecting others from themselves: love refuses to reveal the sinfulness of others. To publicly expose the sins of others indicates a lack of love.

Who will help me? In my shameful state I need a love that throws a garment over of my ugly nakedness—the nakedness I have put on display by my selfish, egotistical, controlling words and choices toward others. Who will protect me if not the members of my own family?

There's a difference between excusing sin and covering it. When the scripture says "*Love covers a multitude of sins*" it does not mean we should ignore sin or treat it like a skeleton in a closet. Loving communities address sinful behavior because it helps bring healing to everyone involved. But the real question is, can I hold others—especially members of God's family—accountable without exposing them to unnecessary shame or ridicule? Galatians 6:1-2 instructs us to both correct the sinner and demonstrate a humble grace: "*If someone is caught in a sin, you who live by the Spirit should restore that person gently. But watch yourselves, or you also may be tempted. Carry each other's burdens, and in this way you will fulfill the law of Christ.*"

Disagreement should never lead to judgment. Not even correction should give us liberty to judge others. It means we learn to love others for simply no other reason than that the Father loves them. It means loving all the church. When I rail against the sins of the church I am simply demonstrating my lack of love for her.

We are each given a stewardship of grace. We can be like the man who foolishly held his one talent and chose not to multiply it. We can keep God's grace to ourselves, or multiply God's grace by extending it to others.

The Enemies of Grace

Grace is abundant and free. It's the deal of a lifetime—no, eternity. When we understand God's grace for what it is, we all want in. Who could be opposed to grace? And yet there are enemies of grace. Even more startling: we ourselves are sometimes the opponents to grace.

Our conflicts with grace are like storm-fronts in our hearts. I've seen a few such storms in my own heart. I wonder if either of these apply to you:

Bitterness

"See to it that no one fails to obtain the grace of God; that no root of bitterness springs up and causes trouble, and by it many become defiled." (Hebrews 12:15) The first enemy of grace is bitterness. The wounded heart draws inward and avoids even grace itself. I want to be alone, alone in my pain. But this aloneness is an illusion. This passage from Hebrews warns us that apart from the grace of God our bitterness and unsettled scores seep into those around us. My bitterness can defile others. We need grace to endure suffering, even in the everyday slights of life. In our pain, when we refuse grace we defile many. All the while we think we are suffering in silence and solitude, unaware that when one member of the body suffers, the whole body is in pain.

Scarcity

"Scarcity" is a terrible word, except that I can think of no other. This second opponent of grace is my fear that grace is a zero-sum game, that grace comes prepackaged in fixed amounts. My mind has yet to inform my heart that his mercy endures forever, and comes in limitless supply. I am the frightened sparrow who thinks his small breaths will consume all the air in the sky. Whatever grace I find I must keep for myself. Who knows where I'll find more? Yet if the Father clothes the flowers of the field and feeds the birds of the air, how much more will he provide the life-giving freedom of grace? Here is the supply of Heaven: when I share the grace I've received, I discover the Source of all grace, who gives the Spirit without limit.

Pride: Also An Enemy of Grace (What—did you think there were only two?)

Four times the scripture teaches us, *"God resists the proud but give grace to the humble."* (Four times!) Among the enemies of grace, human pride hides deepest in our souls. We think grace will expose us as frauds, when all the while grace wants to invite us to a forever feast.

Pride has a thousand faces but always the same dreary aim: to make more of ourselves and less of God. Grace exposes our desire to sit on the throne of our own vainglorious private kingdom. Pride is the leaven of the Pharisees. Pride is an enemy of grace—you can't give grace to people you look down upon; you can only give them pity.

Pride itself has read the Bible, so pride's solution is false humility. False humility is our attempt to fool God. We utter modest things about ourselves we do not believe. The problem with false humility is that it's false. False humility is the self-abasement we want others to reject, thus affirming our talent and skill. C.S. Lewis helps us guard against false humility: "Humility is not thinking less of yourself: it is not thinking of yourself at all."

Pride is always a masquerade. We enter the hall wearing a mask. We receive the praise of men, knowing all along that we look nothing like the costume we wear. Pride leads to the kind hypocrisy where we keenly discern the flaws of others because we are haunted by our own. It makes us seem bigger than we are, and deflates those around us. Because we detest the lies we tell ourselves we try to expose the same lies in others. We hide the very flaws he is willing to love.

The church fathers warned us: possessions lead to pride. In modern times we pretend to joke, "He who dies with the most toys, wins." The ancients reminded us that knowledge puffs up, but love builds up. In modern times we actually believe Knowledge is power. It's not: it leads to pride. Pride leads us in prayer, "I thank you that I am not like other men."

Pride cannot see beyond itself. Pride whispers that if we must accept grace, then we should have it all. Pride is a miser that hoards the grace of God. Pride hoards the grace of God—as if our sin were so great we could consume heaven's full supply of grace, when in fact our sins are common to all mankind. Pride causes us to see grace as a zero-sum game—as if God's kindness to others means less grace for us. But grace is not of this world. It is not scarce; grace is the stuff of the age to come.

Pride harms us deeply; grace heals us utterly. Is it any wonder God resists the proud?

EXERCISE: PULL UP A CHAIR

TAKE TEN MINUTES:

Be still. Invite the Holy Spirit to come near. Breathe.

Get real: Read Colossians 3:1-17. The passage speaks first (vs. 1-8) of dealing with the enemies of grace *within* us. Then look carefully at verses 12-17: do you see the invitation to a grace-filled life lived in Christian community?

Reach Out: It's impossible to live out these verses apart from a life in community with others. Ask God for the practical grace to break free from a life of isolation.

Pray: If you see the need for community, ask the Holy Spirit to reveal your place at the table. Where has God set the table for you? He is faithful: he will lead you home.

Search: Search for your home, your family, and your place at the table. Keep in mind the object of a search is *finding.* Jesus promised: "everyone who seeks, finds."

TAKE A LIFETIME:

Grace grows steady, slow, and sure. The grace of community bears fruit (again and again) after decades of rootedness. Modern life works against this pace.

When Grace Says "Hush"

As the Prodigal son traveled home he prepared a dreadful speech. He no longer wanted to be known as a son. He wanted to live among the servants. He wanted to earn his wage. The Father ignored the speech and interrupted his son by calling for new clothes, the family ring, and lavish feast. The prodigal son never got to the end of that speech. Sometimes the most gracious thing grace can do is tell us to shut up.

God's grace won't allow anyone to speak ill of the family—not even the family members themselves. Grace turns a deaf ear to our self-pity and offers us a banquet of joy. Grace doesn't kill the buzz. Grace doesn't leverage the past in order to get what it wants in the future. Grace does more than live in the moment: it redeems the past, present, and future. It fills every glass and raises a toast to the days ahead. Grace creates a welcome the prodigal will never forget.

Yet grace is not some second-hand Greek god of wine, all celebration and no reflection. Grace is patient and wise in ways we do not expect. Grace is well aware of the years to come, the wounds to mend, and the work of rebuilding a life in the Father's house. After the welcome and after the tears, the deep work of grace begins: learning from the past and shaping the future. There is a time to hear about the days gone by, and when that time comes grace is a good listener. The right time could take weeks or months to surface. It could be over quiet morning coffee or after the children fall asleep. Grace waits for the moment. Grace asks gentle questions, and grace redeems the past and gives hope for the future.

Grace is no mere metaphor: consider the hateful, murderous heart of a man named Saul, who attacked the church of Jesus, imprisoned followers of Christ, and lived a life of religious violence, all in the name of God. Years after the God of grace confronted him on that Damascus road, he spoke of the present and his past:

> *I am the least of the apostles, unworthy to be called an apostle, because I persecuted the church of God. But by the grace of God I am what I am, and his grace toward me was not in vain. On the contrary, I worked harder than any of them, though it was not I, but the grace of God that is with me. (1 Corinthians 15:9-10)*

By grace Paul reflected on what he had done and who he had been. The result was not a past ignored but a life redeemed. This is the way of grace: she allows her guests to choose when and how they will speak of their past. After the shame has subsided and the fear has turned to mist, grace allows us to tell the truth about our past. It transforms secrets into stories of hope. In the quiet moments of grace, you may find your hope for the future buried in the rubble of the past.

Make Every Effort: How We Respond To Grace

Perhaps you're like me: from time to time I catch myself thinking, "If only I had a little more faith I could be a better disciple." Actually, we could substitute nearly any other quality for the word faith: "If only I had a little more teaching, time, energy . . ." Most of us are keenly aware of the qualities we lack as followers of Jesus. We possess the assurance of our weakness instead of the assurance of his faithfulness.

Let me share with you a passage from Peter's second letter that changed my life forever:

"His divine power has given us everything we need for life and godliness through our knowledge of him who called us by his own glory and goodness. Through these he has given us his very great and precious promises, so that through them you may participate in the divine nature and escape the corruption in the world caused by evil desires. For this very reason, make every effort . . ." ~ 2 Peter 1:3-5

When I read this passage several years ago it flashed like lightning across my heart. The thunder still rattles my everyday life. I find seven meditations in these amazing words:

• *"His divine power . . ."* As followers of Jesus, our everyday life in Christ should be based upon his divine power, not our human strength.

• *"has given us everything we need for life and*

godliness . . ." The problem is, most of us think that God did everything on the cross and that's all there is. Good news: he isn't finished dispensing his grace!

• *"through our knowledge of him . . ."* Roadblock—our western mindset leads us to believe that the knowledge of him comes through mere study. A more fruitful approach is to know him by experiencing his presence.

• *"his own glory and goodness. . . "* 21st century Americans have difficulty understanding "glory," but his glory can impact our life—and he is good beyond all measure. Better yet: his glory and goodness are directed toward us!

• *"He has given us very great and precious promises . . ."* Do we ever reflect upon his promises? I'm afraid that for most of us his promises are like autumn leaves: beautiful, but not very useful.

• *"So that through them you may participate in the divine nature . . ."* Here is where the lightning flash knocked me over. We can participate in God's nature, right here, right now. Who knows the full meaning of this phrase? Whatever it means, it has to be good!

• *"and escape the corruption in the world caused by evil desires . . . "* Many believers are trapped into thinking the gospel is only about forgiveness, but the good news is even better: we can be set free from the cycle of corruption!

These are the seven meditations, but there remains one further step. The scripture calls us to action as well:

"For this very reason, make every effort . . ." Notice

that "effort" comes after we encounter his divine power, his glory and goodness, and his precious promises. Too many disciples of Jesus, serious in their commitment to follow him, believe that their effort comes first. Instead, our effort is a response to all he has done.

"For this very reason, make every effort . . ." But there is another segment of Christians who think effort is opposed to grace. For these friends we can only quote Dallas Willard (as we do so often!) "Grace is not opposed to effort, it is opposed to earning."

The challenge of this passage continues into verses 5–11. Wouldn't it be foolish to believe we can accomplish the list apart from his divine power, his glory and goodness, and his precious promises?

How Does Grace Grow?

"God loves me just the way I am." We are comfortable with that statement; we are less comfortable with, "God loves me so much he won't let me stay just the way I am." First his grace saves, then it teaches. We are OK with receiving forgiveness but perhaps skip school when it comes time to learn how to deny ungodliness and worldly passions, and to live sensible and upright lives. Christians can be forgiven if they are confused at this point: week after we week they are told of the complete work of Jesus on the cross, they are told that there is nothing they can do to earn God's approval or salvation. Yet they are also encouraged to live holy lives and keep the commandments, to walk in a manner that pleases God. In most pulpits there is a disconnect between the good news of Jesus' sacrifice and our calling to become the light of the world.

Richard Foster, a man who has spent his adult life encouraging Christians to grow in the grace of God, points out that the message of grace is something more than merely a means for gaining forgiveness. Hearing the same message week after week, along with the same remedy, they remain in the same place. "Having been saved by grace," Foster writes, "these people have been paralyzed by it."

The substance of most evangelical preaching is *sin management* (Willard again) by which Christians find forgiveness apart from the call to come and follow. Since this is all they hear, their expectation of the Christian life is a cycle of sin, forgiveness, and more sin. Perhaps most dangerously, the presence of sin is considered "normal" in the life of a believer. Forgiveness is God's antidote. But what if forgiveness is not the antidote but only the emergency triage? What if there was a cure, a real cure that could go deeper and turn us into the kind of creatures for whom sin is *ab*normal? So many people consider any real attempt at imitating Jesus presumption upon God's grace because we cannot save ourselves through "works." Willard explains that God's grace is not opposed to *effort*, but it is opposed to *earning*. Two pretty different things, aren't they?

This difficulty with grace is the result of decades of emphasis upon his divinity apart from his humanity. Our modern, limited view of grace is directly attributable to the separation we see between Jesus and us. We have been schooled regarding his divinity but the lessons stop with respect to his humanity. Although we may never give voice to the idea, we see Jesus cruising through the challenges of everyday life with the same ease as walking on water. Does your view of Jesus include him as a grace-consumer as well as a grace dispenser?

In liturgical churches the act of receiving the Eucharist is the cleansing moment week by week. Parishioners leave the church in a state of grace fully expecting to fall from that state in the coming days. In evangelical churches the "salvation message" is the staple of preaching week-by-week, coupled with an invitation for believers to come clean with Jesus again and start the week off having received a fresh dose of grace. Whether the grace is administered via the sacrament or through preaching the call to discipleship is not considered a part of that grace. If Christians limit God's grace to mean exclusively the forgiveness of sin, they are locked into immaturity.

If we remain camped at the notion that God's grace is merely another way to describe forgiveness we will never discover that there is grace for everyday living, relationships and ministry to others. In the New Testament alone there are connections between grace and truth, grace and power, grace and spiritual gifts, grace and thanksgiving, grace and generosity, grace and provision, grace and grace and suffering, grace and destiny—and this list is not complete!

Perhaps we are able to recognize the human side of Jesus in the garden of Gethsemane, where he cries out in anguish because of the task ahead. We understand the fear of suffering and the desire to avoid it. We *do* understand why Jesus would say, "Father take this cup from me . . . " but we have no idea how the grace of God helped Jesus to develop into the kind of person who was also able to pray, " . . . yet not my will, but yours be done."

If our view of grace is limited to receiving forgiveness, Jesus cannot be our model for how to receive grace, live in grace, and depend upon grace. Who taught Peter, John, Paul and countless other believers how to live the kind of grace-filled life we see in Acts and the history of the church? How does grace apply to everyday life in a manner that we are conscious of the supply and know how to use it?

The gospels display grace in operation when Jesus was tempted in the wilderness, when he wept at the tomb of Lazarus, even when he drove the merchants from the Temple. He is our model for the operation of grace in times of testing, in sorrow, and in every human emotion we face. He can be the author of such grace toward us, because what he has received he freely shares.

Where Does Grace Grow?

Grace grows in community—but not just any community.

This is a difficult message for many people these days because by *community* I mean *church*. The same Father-God who adopted us into his family intends that we should live together as family. This is a difficult message because in modern times the church of Jesus is largely out of joint. We have created a Christendom where we can choose churches the way most people choose restaurants: according to our individual tastes. By most estimates there are more than 25,000 Christian denominations worldwide. Not individual churches, denominations. How can we grow in grace when we a free to wander from one family to another?

It's an old story. Ask nearly any Christian: you'll hear stories of church drama, church fights, and church splits. But it doesn't have to be like this. Listen carefully the Apostle Peter:

> *Above all, love each other deeply, because love covers over a multitude of sins. Offer hospitality to one another without grumbling. Each of you should use whatever gift you have received to serve others, as faithful stewards of God's grace in its various forms. If anyone speaks, they should do so as one who speaks the very words of God. If anyone serves, they should do so with the strength God provides, so that in all things God may be praised through*

*Jesus Christ. To him be the glory and the power
for ever and ever. Amen. (1 Peter 4:8-11)*

It's easy to miss the word grace in this passage, but you'll find it right in the middle, which is where grace always belongs. Our words and actions are the practical expressions of God's grace. God wants to show his grace through the love, hospitality, encouragement, and service in the community of faith. We extend grace to others precisely because we've received grace from God. Among our families at home—and among the family of God—we are called to be caretakers of grace. Too often we have become merely consumers of grace, and it has led to a church for every taste and preference the consumers can imagine.

One church in my hometown has an interesting way to determine "membership" in the congregation. "If you've hung out with us long enough to have your feelings hurt by someone in the church," says the pastor, "and then decided to forgive and stay here anyway, welcome to the family!" This pastor isn't trying to excuse bad behavior or ignore the flaws of his church, he's trying to playfully indicate that living within a faith community is the perfect opportunity to extend grace to others. Grace grows among family (or at least it should).

Not only does grace grow in the community we call church, it grows in the most unlikely places of the church: among our shortcomings, our hypocrisies, and failings. If everyone in the church had his or her act together, what need would there be to extend grace? Look closely at the passage above: the Apostle Peter

113

calls us to use our gifts in service toward one another. We steward the grace we have received by the way we speak and act toward others in the church.

Have you thought about grace as a stewardship? If not, here's a wonderful exercise: trying reading the parable of the talents (it's in Matthew 25 and also Luke 19) as a teaching about grace. The Master leaves something of great worth with his servants (substitute grace for gold), and when he returns, he looks to see whether we have used his gift wisely.

Best of all of all is our reward. In Matthew's version of the parable, the Master not only praises the good stewards, he extends an invitation: "*Well done, good and faithful servant!*" says the Master. "*Come and share your master's happiness!*" When we distribute the grace of God we will receive his praise, and something more: an invitation to enter into his joy. Through grace, joy increases for everyone.

A Grace Too Small

Here's our problem: we suffer from a grace too small. We've lined up the chairs in neat little rows and called it grace. We never noticed: grace has broken free. Right now it's running wild in the streets. We suffer from domesticated grace. We think grace is pleasant to receive. We think it's ours to give, as if could ladle water from Niagara.

Grace isn't safe: it'll wreck your world. Grace assaults and grace subverts. Grace grabbed one man and knocked him off his ass. It rendered him blind and healed him three days later. Grace put him in danger time and again: shipwrecked three times or more, beaten with rods and sticks, stoned and left for dead. Grace used him like a ragdoll, overthrew an empire, and saved us all—even him, the foremost of sinners.

Grace assaults us in so many ways we are dizzy and dumb from its constant battering. We seldom see it coming, and after it's gone we rarely know what, exactly, just happened. Grace whispers and howls at the moon. Grace asks, and it's the one telling us how it's gonna be. It binds the strongman.

Grace sneaks into a crackhouse and holds the baby in the crib. It breaks into prison and sets the dealer free. Grace says, "*Come, let's reason together*" even when the other side is incapable of true reason. Grace has its reasons of which reason knows nothing.

Grace will pick you up in Kansas and set you down in Oz. You'll pick up crazy friends along the way and

116

discover the boss behind the curtain is just as screwed up as you are. Grace gives you ruby red slippers stolen off a dead woman's feet, and they show you the way home.

Grace is a strong man's game. It's God's game. He invented it and plays it full out. Good luck against God. Grace invites the opponent into the huddle, calls the play, and then runs the ball right up the middle. The enemy knows it's coming, and grace never calls an audible: it executes the play—just try to stop it.

There's only one way with grace. Surrender.

Vagabond Grace

Grace is born in a stable and although it is homeless, it welcomes whoever celebrates its coming. Grace pulls back the veil between heaven and earth; it turns the night sky into the glory of God. Grace is where shepherds dine with Magi and humble young parents play host to perfect strangers. Grace brings together the most unlikely people.

Grace wanders; he does not build a house. Grace searches for welcome. Grace calls at every door, but never trespasses. He stands at the door and knocks, and he's fully prepared to bring a feast inside. Vagabond grace is the beggar bearing treasure. We welcome the wretch into our home; he reaches into his threadbare bag and pulls out gifts more precious than gold. His satchel holds love, joy, and peace. He bestows patience and kindness. He fills the room with the fragrance of goodness, and leaves behind a map to faithfulness, gentleness, and self-control.

Grace is the subtle breath of God clothed in humanity. Grace gives thanks for a humble meal of bread and fish, and thousands sit and eat. Grace suggests a ladle of water can lead to gallons of sweet wine, and then winks a his friends, the only ones in on the jest. Grace never condemns, yet somehow commands us to go and sin no more. Grace walks the pavement and it turns to gold.

Grace supplies our deepest need. We want a deliverer; God sends grace. We want to see power and the glory; God sends grace and truth. We want a king; God sends a servant. Without title or rank, Grace rules the world. Grace has legions at his command, and never once calls for their aid.

Grace is never a tyrant—but forever a king.

Return to Grace

You're in the garden, pulling whatever weeds catch your eye, whichever ones will yield and give way root and all. Head down and sun on your back, you don't even notice the gentle bead of sweat that blooms across your forehead as you work. Then comes a small breeze that brings a soft coolness upon your moist skin. You look up. You see nothing. Renewed and unaware, you return to the task. The returning is grace.

Grace is the breeze that cools. Grace is what only God can do in the midst of your labors. Grace is the whispered word of peace that breathes life into our effort and makes it the work of God. Grace is the calm instead of the storm. Grace comes again and again. It comes so often we think of it as grace returning, but in fact it never left: what comes again and again is our return to grace.

Grace is the foundation of God's work in us, the firm footing from which we can reach and stretch and work and do, the still point that enables any effort--which no effort can improve or change. When the Psalmist urged us, "*Be still and know that I am God*," he did not mean that all our labors would cease, but rather he wanted to remind us that any effort separated from grace is vain effort indeed.

A return to grace is like a return to breathing: grace breathes life in us, a life that we so often take for granted. A return to grace does not mean grace had ever left us at all, only that we become awake to it again. Grace is the atmosphere of our life with God. Each moment it passes through us, unnoticed; yet we would cease to exist without grace. Our great need is to breathe deep of God's inexhaustible gift.

Before we sing God's song we must fill our lungs with grace. In God's kingdom, no matter what we sing, it's in the key of grace.

EXTRAS

GRACE QUOTES TOO GOOD TO IGNORE

"We are born broken. We live mending. The grace of God is the glue." ~ *Eugene O'Neill*

"Grace, like water, flows to the lowest part." ~ *Philip Yancey*"

"I do not at all understand the mystery of grace – only that it meets us where we are but does not leave us where it found us." ~ *Anne Lamott*

Grace is not opposed to effort; it's opposed to earning. ~ *Dallas Willard*

"Humanism was not wrong in thinking that truth, beauty, liberty, and equality are of infinite value, but in thinking man can get them himself without grace."~ *Simone Weil*

"In the New Testament grace means God's love in action towards men who merited the opposite of love. Grace means God moving heaven and earth to save sinners who could not lift a finger to save themselves." – *J.I. Packer*

"Grace saves us from life without God--even more, it empowers us for life *with* God." ~ *Richard Foster*

"God resists the proud, but gives grace to the humble." ~ Proverbs 29:23 *and* James 4:6 *and* 1 Peter 5:5

"All the natural movements of the soul are controlled by laws analogous to those of physical gravity. Grace is the only exception. Grace fills empty spaces, but it can only enter where there is a void to receive it, and it is grace itself which makes this void. The imagination is continually at work filling up all the fissures through which grace might pass." ~ *Simone Weil*

"I rejected the church for a time because I found so little grace there. I returned because I found grace nowhere else." ~*Philip Yancey*

"If a person has grasped the meaning of God's grace in his heart, he will do justice. If he doesn't live justly, then he may say with his lips that he is grateful for God's grace, but in his heart he is far from him. If he doesn't care about the poor, it reveals that at best he doesn't understand the grace he has experienced, and at worst he has not really encountered the saving mercy of God. Grace should make you just." ~ *Timothy Keller*

"If grace is an ocean, we're all sinking." ~ *John Mark McMillan*

"My message, unchanged for more than fifty years, is this: God loves you unconditionally, as you are and not as you should be, because nobody is as they should be. It is the message of grace." ~ *Brennan Manning*

"The beneficiaries of grace should be the benefactors of grace." ~ *Bill Robinson*

THE CONTRAST OF NATURE & GRACE

In his book (written along with Richard Foster) *Longing For God: Seven Paths of Christian Devotion* (InterVarsity Press, 2009), Gayle Beebe provides a list of contrasts between *nature* and *grace*. Beebe offers this list as a guide to journaling and mediation. By his kind permission this list is reproduced in full. He writes:

One of the ways I have found this list helpful is to use it as an interactive guide as I write my journal I have focused on one contrasting day for six thirty-day periods and recorded the results in my journal the effect is staggering.

Nature is crafty and seductive, while grace walks in simplicity.

Nature is self-centered while grace does everything purely for God.

Nature is unwilling to be under a yoke of obedience, while grace moves beyond self-centeredness to minister for God.

Nature works for its own benefit, while grace does not consider how to prosper for its own hands.

Nature willingly accepts honor and respect, while grace attributes all honor and glory to God.

Nature is afraid of shame and contempt, while grace is happy the suffering reproach for the name of Jesus.

Nature is lazy, while grace joyfully looks for something to do.

Nature seeks the unique and different, while grace delights in simple, humble, and even shabby things.

Nature keeps an eye on fashion, rejoices in material gain, and is depressed at loss, while grace attends to eternal things and does not cling to passing ones.

Nature focuses on the body the vanity of life and the worries of self-preoccupation, while grace turns its back on anything that stands in the way of God.

Nature gladly accepts any comfort that gratifies the senses, while grace sinks to comfort in God alone.

Nature is motivated by selfish gain, while grace seeks no reward other than God.

Nature revels in friends and relatives, while grace loves everyone and focuses on the wise and virtuous rather than the powerful and the rich.

Nature turns all things to itself and pushes itself into the spotlight, while grace refers to all things to God.

Nature longs to know secrets and have the inside story, while grace pursues what is useful for the soul.

Nature is quick to complain, while grace endures all things resolutely.

Nature wishes to be seen in public, while grace seeks to avoid vain displays.

Nature longs to be steeped in sensual experience, while grace exercises restraint of the senses.

Nature wants to be noticed by others, while grace wants to be noticed by God.

Nature is ruled by sin, while grace is ruled by grace.

Nature represents vice, while grace represents virtue.

Nature attempts to judge between good and evil, while grace teaches us the eternal law of God.

Nature does not act on what it knows to be good, while grace flees sin and evil.

Nature relies on natural gifts, while grace relies on the gift of God's mercy.

Nature succumbs to vice, while grace radiates virtue.

Nature flees the truth, while grace submits to truth.

Nature runs on its own energy, while grace relies on energy from God.

Nature ignores its failures and refuses to learn from them, while grace humbly embraces shortcomings and learns from them.

Made in the USA
Charleston, SC
16 July 2016